Linda Karshan

marks and moves

Kettle's Yard

11 January - 2 March 2003

Untitled, 1994

INTRODUCTION

*'To go on, and get on, has been my only care. Not always in a straight line,
at least in obedience to the figure assigned to me.'*
Samuel Beckett: *I can't go on. I'll go on*
(A Selection from Samuel Beckett's Work, Grove Weidenfeld, New York 1976)

At first sight it doesn't look as if Linda Karshan's drawings are about the
figure or the body though she insists they are. There is an apparently
abstract drawing, made in 1994, which Karshan even refers to as a self-
portrait. Diagramatically it could be taken as an architect's musing on the
plan for a chapel: white space framed by a pencilled octofoil which has
been emphatically overlaid by a rectangle, pierced on all four sides by
arrow-like angles. Centripetal and centrifugal forces seem to be held in a
tense equilibrium by the strength of its central light.

This was one of the first drawings which Karshan made using a
procedure of marks and moves which has served her purposes ever since.
With the sheet flat on a table or flat on the floor she counts, making
marks, and turns the paper anti-clockwise through 90° on the stroke of 2,
4, 8, or 16, before starting the count again.

Karshan resumed her practice as an artist only in 1983 after seeing
her sons through early childhood and taking a master's degree in
psychology. Drawings from those early months hang in her kitchen at
home and still inform her on a daily basis. One of these, *Untitled, 1983*, is
like an apocalyptic storm in which we struggle to grasp any anchors of
figuration. It's a drawing which seems closest to Jackson Pollock or the
automatic inventions of André Masson or Matta, the Surrealism from
which Abstract Expressionism had emerged via the likes of Arshile Gorky.

Her progress from there on picks up one of the major paths of
twentieth century art: the move away from depiction. Max Morise had
qualified the Surrealists' admiration for the paintings of Giorgio de
Chirico – 'the images are surrealist, their expression is not' – because his
dreams or apparitions were mediated, and therefore distanced and
distorted, through the conventions of illusionistic picture-making.
Ironically, as we have become increasingly aware of the extent to which
meaning derives from language, it would seem that many artists have
wanted to bypass or dispense with language entirely, seeking a more
direct route into our primal, prelinguistic experience.

Untitled, 1983

In this Karshan was helped by her studies in psychology which had focussed on D.W. Winnicott's theory of 'transitional space' through which a child connects its subjective experiences with the reality of the outside, material world. Her dissertation was entitled 'Play, Creativity and the Birth of the Self'. Perhaps unlike the child, however, there is in Karshan a wish also to connect with the greater existence beyond our immediate perception, of which we are aware but which we cannot fully comprehend or relate to by purely intellectual means.

Karshan did not intend to make grids, or stacks or rows. These were the bricks – without the mortar – of '60s and '70s Minimalism. The grid for Sol leWitt or Carl Andre was the ultimately impersonal and egalitarian motif, with no focal point, no part more important than any other, and with the suggestion of being infinitely extendable beyond any given bounds. It was the street plan of the modern city where vistas led off into the New York sky rather than to the monuments of Paris. The Minimalist grid eschewed all self-expression in a play between the idea of something, its physical realisation, our perception of that translation, and the ideas then extending beyond the material fact.

But Karshan's grids, if grids they are, are of a different kind. While Minimalists used rulers and standard units, Karshan, naturally left handed, reverted to using her 'wrong' hand, a practice encouraged by an early teacher, Robert Reed, to avoid all facility and felicity of hand. Her lines are not straight and find their measure from the rhythms of repetition of that simple set procedure of counting and turning, at first from the head but then emanating from deep within her body. Indeed the lines seem to have their own natural inflection and 'lean', and are tempered by intuitive variations of speed and pressure.

The drawings are not planned except that, despite being drawn on the flat and turned, they are destined to end up hanging vertically and 'portrait' shape, subject to the laws of gravity, though defying them, and confronting us bodily. More often than not a drawing starts with a mark, up and left of centre, at its 'heart', and then begins to grow as the body and, progressively, the drawing itself begin to take control. Marks form rectangles which form columns and rows, teetering on the edge of instability. At any moment a 'brick' might fall from a horizontal 'stack' and the whole drawing will collapse. They are unpredictable, and frequently fingerprints or even shoe-prints remain as active reminders of the creative dance. Sometimes, even, their debt to Surrealism can surface in chance traces of frottage from the top of the drawing table now encrusted with a decade and more of graphite.

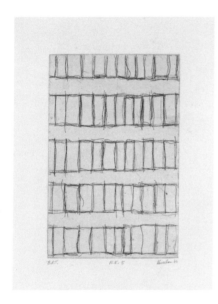

For all the simplicity of the most recent drawings, there is an intensity and urgency and a sense of exultation to the activity and to each drawing she allows out of the studio. In the early mark and move drawings there was often a play, even a struggle, between the straight and the curved, the square and the round. Now curves seem to be subsumed (though not suppressed) within the 'straight' lines. The sense of light has also changed, no longer beaming through from behind the drawing but integral to it. Sometimes the gaps between the ends of lines create magnetic fields of light. Elsewhere light appears to emanate from the way in which those unstraight lines, of different speeds and modulation, manipulate the space they divide or enclose.

And in these recent times ventures into printmaking have fed back into the drawings, from the finest filigree of an etched or drypoint line to the determined carving of a woodblock. For while Karshan draws and only

N.E.5, 2002, etching

draws (if we include printmaking), her drawings, in their physical acknowledgement of their two-dimensional state, are more the drawings of a sculptor than a painter.

Back in 1994, Karshan found affirmation for her method of counting and turning when she first saw Samuel Beckett's teleplay *Quad* at the ICA, and Beckett has never been far away in the ensuing years. The similarity of that 1994 'self-portrait' drawing to the plan of a chapel could be felt as an individual's echo of a medieval cathedral, built as a projection of the body of Christ, as a mediator between us and the whole of creation. Karshan goes on, 'at least in obedience to the figure assigned to me', and, as she heard the 83-year-old dancer Merce Cunningham say last year, 'the rhythms keep on coming – they just do'.

Karshan's London studio is spacious, sparse and tidy, with only the things necessary for work. But among the necessities there are some books, annotated and underlined when something strikes a chord, and this passage she has transcribed into a notebook:

' They told me that the truth of the universe was inscribed into our very bones. That the human skeleton was itself a hieroglyph. That everything we had ever known on earth was shown to us in the first days after death. That our experience of the world was desired by the cosmos, and needed by it for its own renewal.'
Saul Bellow, *Something to remember me by*, Collected Short Stories, edited by Janis Bellow, Viking/Penguin.

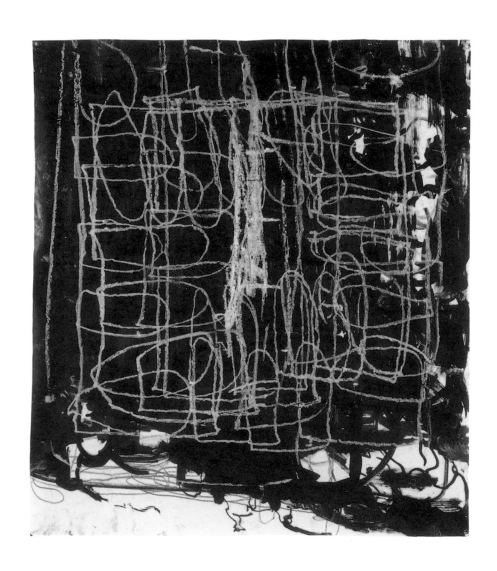

Untitled VII, 1994

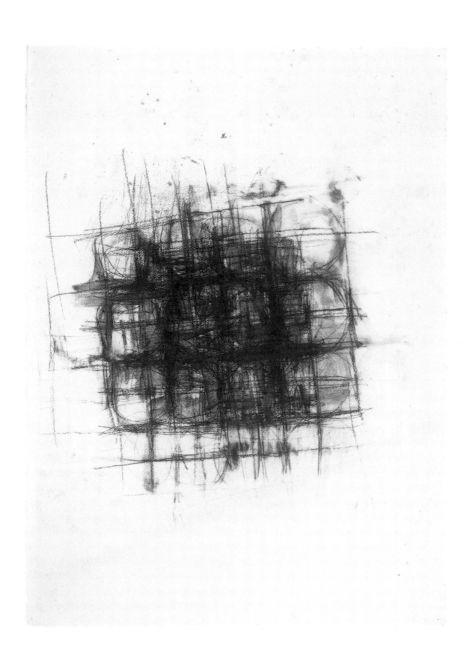

Untitled (August), 1996

Untitled, 20/9/1999

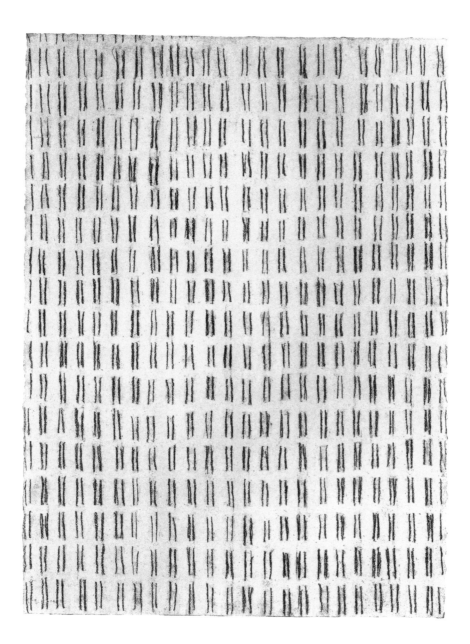

Untitled, 28/1/2000 - 15/2/2000

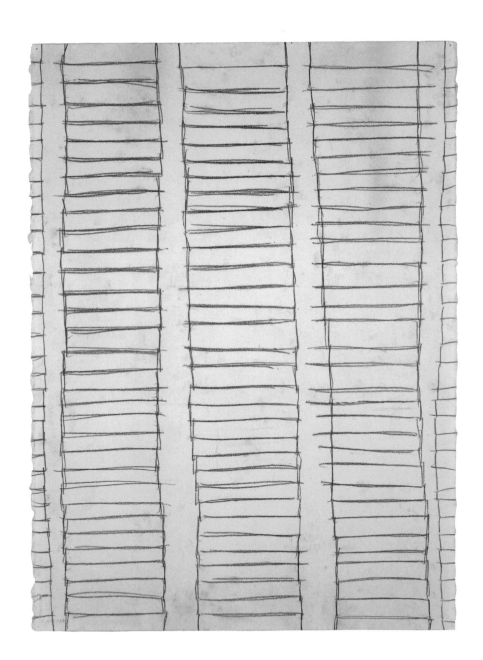

Untitled, 26/7/2000

Untitled, 6/8/2000 (I)

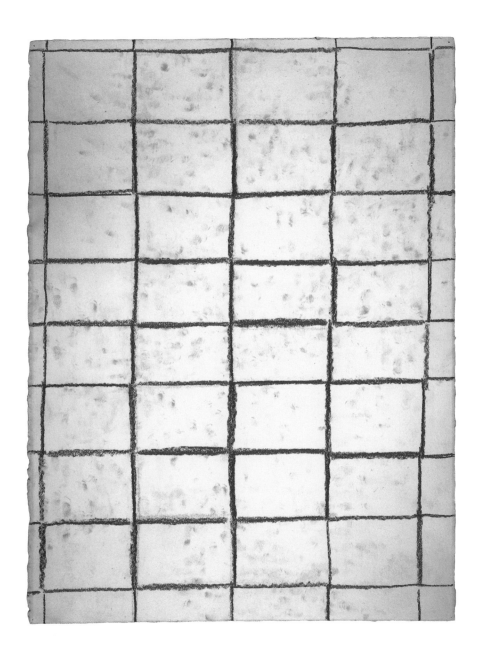

Untitled, 15/10/2002

Untitled, 17/10/2002

Untitled, 1/8/2002 (I)

Untitled, 5/8/2002 (II)

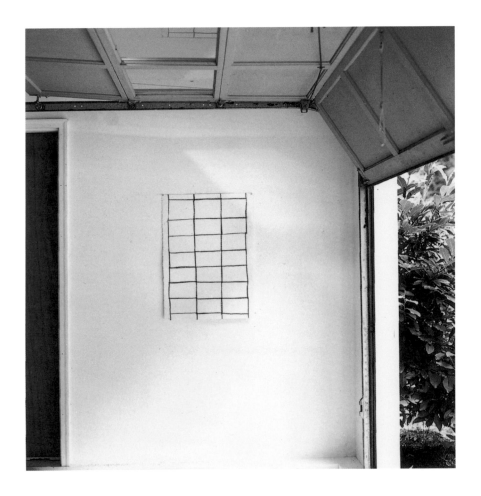

The Connecticut studio (photo: Iraida Icaza)

Untitled, 28/8/02 (II)

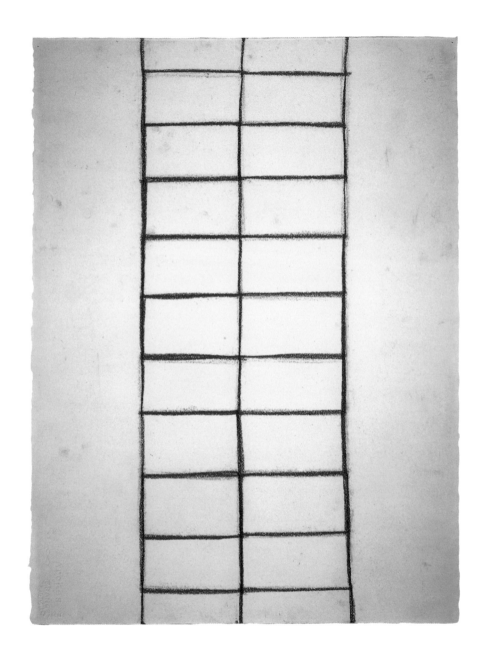

Untitled, 30/7/2002 (IV)

Untitled, 6/8/02 (IV)

The Connecticut studio (photo: Iraida Icaza)

TELLING THINGS TO THE ANGELS:

Linda Karshan at Kettle's Yard

One year ago, Linda Karshan's drawings were shown at the Soane Museum in London, and in the statement she wrote for the exhibition catalogue the artist pointed out an affinity she felt her work had with the labyrinthine nature of Sir John Soane's house, describing the importance that the maze or labyrinth plays in the conceptual origins of her work. Finding a way through the labyrinth is a journey that takes place in the mind, but is also reflected in the steps, the rhythmic pacing around the sheet of paper that conditions the process whereby the artist places the marks on the sheet. It is this process that makes Linda Karshan's drawings such a direct, unmediated, expression of her artistic idea. It gives ample allowance for chance or accident in the marks on the paper, while the element of control is provided, not by a subject nor by the demands of abstract form, but by a rhythmic series interpreted physically by the artist herself.

At Kettle's Yard there are again strong connections between Linda Karshan's work and the 'idea' of the house and its collection, as well as close affinities with many of the works that make it up. Jim Ede, the moving spirit of the place, intended to create not an art gallery or museum, nor a collection reflecting his own taste or the taste of his time, but, as he wrote in 1970, 'a continuing way of life from these last fifty years, in which stray objects, stones, glass, pictures, sculpture, in light and in space, have been used to make manifest the underlying stability which more and more we need to recognise if we are not to be swamped by all that is so rapidly opening up before us.' Linda Karshan's artistic practice, a continuing way of life in the deepest sense, with its foundations in philosophical thought and its awareness of millennia of creative activity, is in harmony with these aims.

Kettle's Yard made a very direct and unexpected impact upon me
when I first visited the house some twenty years ago. I was confronted
with the most powerful expression of an aesthetic that had been part of
my life since childhood, and if I make a personal digression here, it is
because there is still, I believe, a widely shared and deep appreciation for
the artistic sensibility that is represented here. Materials and the
immediacy of the artists' and craftsmen's engagement with them are
paramount. The colours of wood and clay, together with the transparency
of glass and the northern light, predominate. It is a sensibility of the north
(Linda Karshan, let us not forget, is from Minnesota), which embraces the
bleached colours of winter – if sometimes hankering for the warm colours
of the south – and it is a sensibility that certainly infuses much of the best
British art of the past century. My mother, Dora Raeburn, spent some

Kettle's Yard (photo: Harry Sowden, from A Way of Life)

forty years of her life making a home for a husband and seven demanding children, but at the beginning and the end of her life she was an artist, primarily a painter. Throughout all this time, however, she created an environment in our home where fabrics, furniture, pictures, pottery, and everything for everyday use or for decoration had to pass a kind of test: garishness, extravagance, poor design, ugly materials simply didn't appear. It was the antithesis of kitsch, but none the less joyful and exhilarating for that. Kettle's Yard, when I first went there seemed to take this ideal still further, and also to include paintings and drawings by artists whose work we could only see in museums. From then on, wherever I was, every room, every object, every work of art could be classified as 'KY' or 'not KY'; this was a game, of course, but one that acknowledged both Dora and Kettle's Yard. Kettle's Yard is much more than a house filled with art: in his appreciation of every surface or texture in light and dark, and in his arrangement of pictures, furniture, sculpture, pottery and glass, objects, stones, Jim Ede created his own oeuvre, a serial work to be endlessly rediscovered.

My earliest encounter with the work of Linda Karshan produced a similarly unexpected and thrilling sense of familiarity. Even before one is aware of the almost ritualistic procedures by which the drawings are produced, it is apparent that they are not simply fabricated by the artist but are imprinted with her practice and her presence. Jim Ede wrote of rooms that he believed 'the one thing a human being really needed was a room to live in, and scarcely any human being lived in one, it lived on him.' It is in a similar sense that Linda Karshan lives in her art. 'In her daily practice, the artist encounters herself. So does the viewer.' (Tadashi Otsuro) It is, I suppose, this sense of a living presence in the drawings that produces at first sight a sense of recognition, a sense that they are part of the natural world. In Ede's book A Way of Life, he reflects on a photograph of floorboards with the shadow of a chairback in a bright shaft of sunlight:

'I often think that such a fleeting moment as this is even more important than the paintings and sculpture, for it is this which brings inspiration to the artist. On the other side, were it not for the vision of the artist revealing such beauty, we might never see it. It is I suppose this natural interaction and interrelation which is at the root of life's joy. As I look at these floorboards in the photograph they become intensely a part of myself: cracks, notches, joins, the passages of darkness and the transparency of shadow, here perceived, create something which I had not reached when I walked across them. It is this, I think, that Rilke means when he writes that we are here to tell things to the angels; that as created beings we have this perceptive power and that it calls out to be used.'

One of the joys of Kettle's Yard is the lack of distinction between the paintings and sculptures of artists who include Miró, Braque, Ben and Winifred Nicholson, Christopher Wood and Henri Gaudier-Brzeska, the naive paintings of Alfred Wallis and Bryan Pearce, the variety of man-made objects, the fabric of the house itself, and the shells, seed pods and stones arranged by Jim Ede – most notably the famous spiral of almost spherical stones diminishing in size from the centre. Linda Karshan's rejection of painting for the 'rigour of drawing and print-making' is a decision that seems entirely in harmony with the ethos of Kettle's Yard. Indeed, the sequential nature of her work based on a procedure of repetition, which makes each individual drawing or print a reflection of the archetypal oeuvre, has affinities with the work of a potter like Lucie Rie, four of whose bowls are in the Kettle's Yard collection, bought when exhibitions of her work were put on in the gallery during the 1970s. The combination of great refinement and the immediate physical impact of the artist's hand is common to the work of both artists, as is the cool sensitivity to their materials and the fusion of accident and intent. Lucie was a dear friend of Dora Raeburn's and, perhaps since her work was common to both Dora's and Jim Ede's collections, she has always seemed to me the height of KY. There is no doubt that Linda's work belongs in this same select company. So many things that Jim Ede wrote about the art and the objects he loved seem to have an appositeness to her work, for at its heart his was an attitude that looked for the transcendental in simplicity:

'It is salutary that in a world rocked by greed, misunderstanding and fear, with the imminence of collapse into unbelievable horrors, it is still possible and justifiable to find important the exact placing of two pebbles.'

Michael Raeburn

N.E. I, 2002, etching

N.E. II, 2002, etching

BIOGRAPHY

Linda Joseph, was born in Minneapolis to a family of Romanian Jewish origin. She studied fine art at Skidmore College in New York State from 1965-66 with the architect Robert Reed, a former student of Josef Albers at Yale, and then for a year read art history at the Sorbonne, specialising in Surrealism. In 1968 she married New York television executive Howard Karshan. Since 1969 they have lived in London where they brought up two sons, Roger and Tommy, born in 1973 and 1976. During the early '70s Linda entered Jungian analysis and started to practise Pilates, an exercise regime involving positioning of the body and spatial awareness, which she still continues. In 1983 she completed a Master's degree in Humanistic Psychology on the Antioch University (Ohio) programme in London, before returning to drawing.

Her working year is divided between studios in Denmark Hill, London and Connecticut. Since 1995 she has produced several series of etchings and drypoints, working with Todd Norsten in Minneapolis, and has recently worked on etchings and woodcuts at Hope (Sufferance) in Camberwell. She exhibits regularly with Galerie Biedermann in Munich and the Redfern Gallery in London. In 2001 she exhibited at the Soane Museum in London and was given a major retrospective at IVAM in Valencia.